Turn on the Dark

JOHN ELIOT

MOSAÏQUEPRESS

First published in 2018

MOSAÏQUE PRESS
Registered office:
70 Priory Road
Kenilworth, Warwickshire
CV8 1LQ

EDITOR OF THIS COLLECTION: Paola Fornari

ISBN 978-1-906852-44-3

Printed and bound in the UK.

For my wife, Jill.

Contents

Preface

I think about death more and more as I get older.

On the recommendation of a friend, I read *Staring at the Sun* by the psychiatrist Irvin Yalom, in which he presents his ideas to help people face death. The book is not simply for those who are terminally ill, but for anyone at any age.

Yalom writes that usually it's older people who fear death: they fear death when they retire, when they recover from a serious illness, or when contemporaries begin to die off.

I fear death.

I am haunted by the memory of the time when my phone beeped at 5am and the message from my daughter read, "I'm sorry, Dad, but I've just heard that Leonard Cohen has died." My wife was away, I was alone in the darkness of a breaking dawn, the street was silent as I listened to an old record, and Leonard haunted my morning. This man I had never met had been a part of my life since I was fifteen, and now was no more.

The people I miss most who have died were not blood related: Cohen, my step-grandpa and my dog. Oscar Wilde wrote, "A dog takes your heart and then breaks your heart."

These poems are a therapy; certainly a therapy for me, and perhaps also for you, the reader. I hope so.

– John Eliot, Cardiff, 2018

Acknowledgements

This is my third collection. It would not have been possible without the inspiration, encouragement and help of others.

My grandchildren had a direct influence on some of the poems. Since my second collection was published, I have a new granddaughter. I am now the grandpa of Cameron, Carlton, Scarlett, Lilwen and our newest arrival, Mila.

There are others to thank. Editor and proofreader Paola Fornari: words cannot describe how I rely on her. Paola makes me think so much about what I've written as well as making sure the semi-colons are in the right place.

I thank my brother, Haydn, for teaching me how to read poetry.

I thank all those who give me the opportunity to read my poetry in public.

And as always, I thank my wife, Jill, to whom this collection is dedicated.

– JE

Time wasted, treading
an empty room
windswept autumn, bare trees
forgetting the green. Spring Summer Winter.
Haunted. Waiting for voices. Sing in harmony.

Death Rebirth

Where are remains of dead
corpses that once were living?
Gone through the passage
of yellow-breasted spirit?
She taps her beak on doorway
to world throat's grave
birth in reverse.

2017-18

Melody of the Bird

How the birds sing along.
They always knew the song; melody
before you set it free
in a garden, easy.
Scorched lawn.

You are burning already.
You fear the sounds.
You feel like the only person alive.

When you greet your dead husband
say hello from me.

2017-18

Autumn
(For Elizabeth Barrett Browning)

The cricket grinds, sings as a mandolin.
Then silence. She does not even call within
eve of desolation, lost as her voice echoes.
I hear her weeping.
Then sing for me before emptiness
and silent winds blow.

2018

Fishermen

Do you remember
when the North Sea froze?
Death to samphire
on Norfolk coast.

Lone scarecrow, straw
ragged, bleeding skin, raw
as blue marble waves
lay shallow still
and iced white sand,
six point crystal.

Silence swept the shore
to three fishermen
watching seas from sheds;
warmed by braziers
waiting for the thaw.

2015-18

Ten Years Old

Mary, amongst all women blest,
holier than the rest.
Whispered echoes window vaults
moonlight luminous halo holds the innocence.
He knows all,
my thoughts send me to hell.

There hangs a crucifix
—died for us all, Gran tells me—
bought from a monk at Mount St Bernard
with a vial of Pope blessed water.
I lie, eyes fixed to the nightmare;
the cross holds a man. Tortured and pinned.

Shivering beneath the eiderdown,
television playing softly;
I hear hushed conversation of Grandma, Grandpa;
smell secure comfort of Woodbine
drift upstairs
across the landing,
like sweet incense.

1963:
I fear sleep's ghosts
like religion.
But night takes me
to a new day,
resurrected.

2013-18

The Kiss

A man whistles an up-tempo beat
that doesn't fit his suit.

For nineteen months
and two weeks he hasn't
been kissed
full on the mouth.

But then
he feels her lips
her breath like fresh rain
her eyes black, stark,
reflecting the poem to be written.

2017-18

She

Eyes
stark as a flower's
purple iris

stare at the beholder.
The iris knows my name
knows my mind.

Knocks at my door
all night long
gifting me her perfume.

Just if she did,
if she did just that.

Don't sit at my mirror
conspiring with your hair
leading me to temptation.

My naked iris.

2017

Saturday Afternoon Mahler

Venice and
we could have died joint suicide
1973:
the memory of her
lost in my arms
hair black and unbrushed
sleeping after love.

So long ago
long ago from cacophony
she sang the fifth Adagietto
like the beauty of the morning bird
flying to the nearest cloud.

2017

Looking for Alyson

Insecure only what is felt.
Last night is passion spent;
some drunk's empty pocket.

Out of control
me over you.
I thought you were for real
I thought you were for real.

I've begun again
reborn into different love.

Love is only the mistakes we make
learning to
love again.

Looking for Alyson.
Talking Lou Reed to
a junk.

Lonely house. Empty bedroom
your clothes need you here
sweat warming me
clinging to the bed we shared.

A time she smiled
my life was nearly complete.

Loneliness is a nightmare.
I call. Do you hear?

1998-2018

Saturday Morning

She buys her own flowers.
Paints her clouds blue.
Says to the sun,
Wish I were you.

2014

Saturday Afternoon

He always bought fresh flowers
though there was
no one
in his life.

Men in the bar laughed,
felt big.
They had someone
to go home to:

flowerless wives,
demanding children;
the burden.

While he alone listened
to silence
watching flowers wilt.

1995-2018

Chennai Summer

Sounds of the street,
0548 in another country.

Horns sound
from dawn to dusk

dusk to dawn
with lingering sigh.

At the darkest hour for a few minutes
silence

but for the whirr of the fan
and air con

sounding like waiting.
Still cool rain

2015

Ratna Café

South India coffee
tastes fresh
as morning street sounds
in the café

from the road
where people
walk the pavement
passing
a cowbell rings

heard just
for a moment
before horns

engines turn
diesel fumes
mix the steam of coffee
essence of memory

2015

First Birthday

Red wearing your party
dress. One end of your
life to another. Fear
chills your smile
to faces surrounding.
Do you realise
what fate
awaits?

2015

The Eve of Execution:
Thoughts of Lady Jane Grey

Stars stand still;
shine daytime. Let me
fly blue sky as white swans
leave feathers burning.
Let me lie on the hillside,
ask the grass,
"Where do you leave your scent?"
Let me become one with
flight as a night creature
hidden within the ghost.
Stones of history.
Grey and empty.

2016

Three Lilies

Who is that passing
resting on the arm of love?
Hear a voice.

"Come away
winter has gone; the rain has passed."

"Three lilies sing as a choir;
lilies of the field dressed in white and gold. Remember?
We heard them."

"Now they are silent.
Still as wheat without a breeze."

"Leave the lilies.
It's not about present
but future.
That is where you find poetry,
poetry of song.
Bird of grey dawn sing to us.
Love, strong as death.
Anger, fierce as the grave.

We will hear them again."

2018

Prime
I

Silence rewinds, watch time
as stars blacken the frame
exiting, fading before break of day.
Wait, words to end the world.
Mouth, meditation, my heart
accept the night, take this hour.
Where are streaks of red
this grey clouded dawn? Mist covers the valley.
Hear me.

Hear my cry for the burden I carry.
Bush of thorns, I wait in your shadow
search for your fruit.
Satisfy my hunger, one purple berry.
Satisfy my thirst flesh for juice;
blood breaking, gifting freedom
exiting eternal wheel of death. I wait.
A whisper, only a whisper.

A warm blush of breeze
passes quickly. Let it sleep
fade and watch slowly
as sweet nectar
from a swarm of bees
gone, breath and life.
Memory sings. Melody without key.
Sorrow, a leaf fallen from trees.
Footprints vanished from sight
as birdsong echoes in the night.

2017-18

Prime
II

Morning tolls
seven minutes past seven bells

with red sun swiftly risen.
Soundtrack to daybreak

over lush green fields
staring without blindness,

strength of white campion:
heaven's star of dawn.

2018

Listen

We waited for rain
from red yellow
vault, losing its lights,
as arid sun
rose over horizon.
We were in heaven;
stillness before sound of angels against the pane:
celestial bells.

2017

Arvo Pärt

I smell heat on stone.
Sound the bell of ancient time
as the priest intones spirits from a distance.
Watch the moon swell towards dusk
in this Estonian sunset.
No artist plays an old melody,
homage to beauty
of red streaks against darkening sky.
Lone star hangs as laughter echoes through my dreams.

Dark ends before dawn;
I freefall and wake
with graceful arc
of the night owl
as blood blends,
I find
we are one.

On the boat to a far land
laughter of seas;
remember day already lost,
heat too oppressive
people too foreign.
Walking on a film set
no beach to receive it.
How can this grain of sand support deep sadness?
Try to remember

I could have murdered on the beach;
stranger and absent beggar.
Boats lie empty in the sun

waiting for tomorrow's catch.
How lonely can a fishing net be?
And then,
the temple unreal

take me with you
take me to the wind,
to the soft breeze
and so by the way
let us travel to the sky
tell the butterfly
give me back my wings
I can give you my voice
teach you to sing
lying still tasting nectar
from blue within gold
beauty of the flower
why would you want to fly
in blissful heaven lie and die

Where to? The sea asked me.
Where will you take these words?
Shadows that gleam under
steps of sad passengers
write eternal melancholy
with their lonely melody.
But the red street sound doesn't answer.
Only echoes on marble.

2017-18

Praying Mantis

Shade from the heart
as storm against a wall,
heat in a dry place.

Hear the mantis pray
and Catholic bell.
Violin without harmony of angels.

Look to the sky, blue
silently becoming grey.
Wait for downpour,
knowing all will be no more.

Quench my thirst
wine on the lees.

2018

Grasshopper of the Inner Voice

Looking for you
edge of the garden
entering this or next world.
Hearing a voice unknown.
Seeing yellow scented flowers
feeding their nectar grief of grey clouds
droplets where sunshine breaks through.
Red orange yellow green blue indigo blends the passion,
holds a grasshopper
clings to my ankle. Calling out,

"I was alone without the unity,
without the three, without The One."

2018

Birth

Hear breath
first breath.

Expected, unexpected divine sent chord.
Hear music!
Sound pulsating
swept over space
until imagination knows no difference
between call and silence.
Music Sunday
not hymns or church
bells of mourning long past.
Hear the dead, unheard in prayer.
Look into any
window. A ghost would see a figure listening
music from another place;
memory of beginning.
Is it the opening passage?
Though of destination

cut. Before the start
a broken bell

waits, then sounds;
music plays without flow,
no water to swim

or drown.

Night travel, silence
without leaving, fearing
journey's end.
Life as a hanged man,
lost. Amongst all discordant notes
pining for the melody
a lullaby,

a grandma to cling to.
But a tin drum, tuneless piano,
sing the children to sleep.

Those lost children
wander the room of toys

shake fists at the universe
becoming an electric star sound.

Listen quietly;
hear breath hear breath.

2018

The Angel

I sit looking to distant land,
curve of the sea, waves
gentle against sand
shimmer into sun.
Rainbows of butterflies cast shadows
circling from wings;
fading into evening.

An angel walks the hill
to rest by my side.

"Let's leave,"

"Where?" I ask.

"To the shore,
the next world."

"And, if I go with you
through the open door?"

"An entry. Not an exit.
Life changes. Life moves.
We walk on the edge of time.
Watch. Listen. Silence tells all."

2018

Death

"If I am taken
as I stand here
to plain crossed branches,
Naked Serpent hidden in my crown
listens to the wind that blows from across universe long ago.
Cold. Cold I feel a shiver,
tender as the touch of Eve, naked as Adam.
Limbs are a stark soul.
The Devil scares young and old."

Crowded Saturday street stands
Death;
shrouded stretched flesh
over bones.
Hollowed orbits
speak reflecting words
scattered around a grave.
Who is born
wanting to be a corpse?
Where is the body and life
blood wafer
and wine?

2017-18

Sound of the Thin Curved Horn
Asks, 'Who has Died Tonight?'

Death's key holds no memory
for waiting seabed souls.

No metempsychosis
for those drowned in screams

as the one
who is dead.
has been forgotten
hearing many whispering
in silence.

Bones waste away;
go about as a shadow.
Like the stillborn
who never sees the sun;
sees the moon
and licks the dust.

In the house of the dead
a single bell echoes
at the end of the terraced street.

Cranes hang over the Tyne
into the sliding sunset like
a life measured in squares.
The wake sits, waits for something
something to happen.

Eternity comes to a full stop
after sixteen minutes and one second.

Lamps shine. Streets belong where
they follow cracked pavements;
there are words to be read, a cracked reflection.
Touch on shoulder, turn,
is there no one in this forest of demolition
to watch, to care?
Star, slivered silver moon;
universe give me your life, the warmth.
Pass a shadow. Nightmare
loneliness of a tune
one stringed violin.
Hear voices speak, the dancers drag

a leaden coffin
behind them death,
seventh seal. The burden knowing

where to be born, when to die.

2017-18

Resurrection

Wet, like rain on footsteps, footprints
against arid sand where
blood has not breathed for the length of universe
at world's edge;
creation has died, waiting
for the spirit to speak: "Let there be"
there was light and with the light came
the above and below
firmament
and earth
clouds gathered
water cascaded.
From the clay rose resurrected and felt
wet, like rain on footsteps.

2018

Marianne

Without her there
would not have been the song.
Marianne wrote the words.

She was the Indian cotton
and patchouli
empty bedsits where

I still listen
for your step on the stair.
How many poems today

from lovers as old
and sad as me
end as you with the words

so long?

28-07-16

Friday Night Song

Too early
for your death
this cold dark dawn.
I am alone but for Friday night songs
and lost passion. Your voice,
sing me in this empty house;
whistling life away
to the final notes.

Softly as in morning sunrise

cold morning light
after deep night.
I'll never know but
remembering you leaving,
silent as light disappearing,
suicide of sunset.

07-11-16

Last Words from the Grandchildren

Imagine riding on the sun.
Travel speed of light. As day ends
turn on the dark;
watch the trees peel apart.

2018

End

Stop.
Silence and all that remains.

2018

THE AUTHOR, John Eliot, was born in Leicester. He taught in the south-west of England before moving to France with his wife to write full-time. He now divides his time between France and Wales. His first collection of poetry, *'Ssh,* was published by Mosaïque Press in 2014; his second collection, *Don't Go*, followed in 2016. His novel *The Good Doctor* was published in 2014.

www.ingramcontent.com/pod-product-compliance
Lightning Source LLC
Chambersburg PA
CBHW060542030426
42337CB00021B/4402